Until I met Black Men

HOPE GISELLE

print ISBN: 978-1-66780-112-4

ebook ISBN: 978-1-66780-113-1

DEDICATION:

These words are for the black boy I thought I had to be and the black man I never became. These words are for the black women scarred by the patriarchy, searching for a home in a version of feminity we were never meant to attain to validate men who don't often value our greatness enough to say thank you for our mere existence. These words are for the black men I have loved and lost. I say to those men, "I'm sorry," "thank you," and you're welcome. These words are for the black men on a mission to be the most authentic version of themselves despite the status quo. This book is dedicated to my father, Mr. Roosevelt Hadley. You saw me before I saw myself and made me promise to be just that, and I will always love you for it. These words are for the black women who affirm my womanhood and acknowledge that I am still your sister as different as we are; I am still your sister.

PREFACE :

I explored the contents of this book while navigating questions around who I was as a woman. You all are about to read a bit of my personal story and understanding what it means to be a black man in society and what it means to navigate them while being a woman of a specific life experience. Navigating these words was not easy, and to be quite frank with you, being able, to tell the truth, based on my own logic and understanding of black male hood after rejecting my own, is sure to get me backlash. I am prepared to tell this truth by setting women like myself free and men like those mentioned into a space of forwarding momentum in their personal lives and journeys.

FOREWORD:

I am a Black cisgender woman who has never fully questioned what it means to be Black and/or cisgender and/or female. I am old enough to be Hope Giselle's Mama. Yet, no part of my identity has ever truly been questioned or investigated in the manner in which she investigates her own identity and the men she has encountered in her book "Until I Met Black Men."

I grew up safely as a young Black middle class girl in Atlanta, Georgia in the late 1960s through the 1970s. When I say I grew up "safely," I mean that I had a Mama and a Daddy who loved me and provided for me in a Black neighborhood and in Black communities where I never wondered or questioned who I was or who I belonged to. That might sound like some foreign concept in the year 2021, but that was my truth. It would take me decades into my adulthood before I recognized that being Black and female was something that did not always sit well with white folks and, occasionally, with some Black folks.

The word "transgender" was not a part of any Black parlance that I knew of back then. I certainly heard the terms "Sissy" and "Dyke" applied to a variety of folks that did not always neatly fit the implied definitions. My late Mama simply called all of the folks conveniently crammed into these varied definitions "different." I wish I could summon her wisdom now. My late Mama was a schoolteacher who had a simple philosophy that emphasized that all of us had a particular gift that we were endowed with. It did not matter what package we arrived in, we just simply arrived on this planet with whatever the Creator gave us. Our job was simply to use and develop whatever the Creator gave us to make life better for ourselves and for all of those folks that we encountered on that journey called "life."

Hope Giselle has written yet another work about her identity as a Black woman, an identity shaped in large part, for better or worse, by her encounters with Black men and with concepts of how masculinity and manhood is formed in the Black community. If truth be told, the concept of what is and is not feminine is also shaped by those concepts. Therein lies part of the problem...

Black manhood—whatever the hell it is or is not—is both a tool and a weapon, depending on where you are standing. Black womanhood, particularly Black transgender womanhood, often appears to folks who don't look too closely, as a rejection of Black manhood when it is not. Hope Giselle's self-evaluation then, is not simply another memoir of her coming to terms with being a Black transgender woman. It is also a deeply personal exploration of how she arrived at her own definition of what it means to be a Black woman. That exploration is her gift to us...

© Leslye Joy Allen, Historian

CONTENTS

"I have learned over the years that when one's mind is made up, this diminishes fear; knowing what must be done does away with fear."

Rosa Parks

CHAPTER 1:

EXPECTATION:

There's a science to understanding what it means to love, like, care for, and share space with black men. There's an internal understanding of the pain you're expected to endure for the sake of his greatness and will-shattering patience you must have to move into moments that provide you peace. So, what happens when you realize that the relationships you held so tightly to your chest had become nothing more than dissertation-like thoughts to be unpacked and then restocked in the shelf of your existence? How do you move beyond your visceral pain to create room for what it means to be a black man in America? Hell, what is it even like to be a black man in America when black men don't even get to decide what their masculinity is anymore?

I know a few folks who are familiar with me and find themselves confused at my disassociation from male-hood, but I assure you that I have known very little of what it truly means to be a black man. I do, however, know what pressures expectations can create. I understand what it is to be a boy, a black boy beyond the blue lights and the coke lines on my dining room table. I know what it's like to be expected to hold back the tears you deserve to cry because your environment is a factory, and you are the product. The demand for your failure is high, and the supply is abundant with folks who believe that the assembly line is their way out because a black man told them that the conveyor belt to heaven was paved in toxicity.

I know what it's like to pray. To ask for forgiveness for not wanting to become the Black man that everyone else needed you to be. To watch the blood pour from your forehead down the bridge of your nose and through your lips, as the crystal case that inflicted the pain is washed and placed back in its original position, only to try and forget it was ever used as the object of a traumatic experience.

I knew so much and still knew nothing at all because I wanted to remain blind. I wanted an excuse to hate the thing that I was expected to become. I knew nothing of self-love; I resonated with the thought of hating myself because I had two strikes against me before I ever became Hope, and the black men in my life never let me forget it. They never let me forget that my purpose was to bottle my joy and sip it slowly, but never from a straw. I was taught to manage my manhood like a hostage negotiator in a high-risk situation, to microdose the micro-aggressions I would face from folks who would view me as a threat based on nothing other than my existence. I would've been the black man that knew too well what it meant to be completely content with the storyline of a character whose life I was expected to play. I was expected to tell the story regardless of my time, trying to get away from the idea that I needed more. I would've been okay with being mediocre for the sake of being the type of black man that made everyone proud. I would've done what needed to be done; only when I had finally had enough of the charade would the world have made space for me to atone for the harm I'd caused in the process of fulfilling my duty?

I'd have the opportunity to be forgiven because I was a black man, but I never became one. I never got the chance to harness the privilege of manhood. I never knew what it was to woefully access my perceived "power" over women or the black family, due in large part to my disgust with the notion that my ownership of a penis and acceptance of manhood afforded me the right to stand in spaces that I wasn't qualified for based on a system and social order that I didn't understand.

I knew nothing. I understood very little, but I did understand the things that I had to control. I had to hold my mannerisms and parts of my body language. I had to be mindful of how my hands fell in times of rest. I had to be conscious about my skin color and what that said about the type of man I could be. The man that I was supposed to be was never the man that I resonated with. Parts of me fell in love with the idea of the toxic role because the parts of me that were finding myself falling in love with the idea of being suitable to love someone who was what I was trying to get away from. As cliche as it might be, I wanted to fall in love with the men who reminded me of most of the things that I despised about men. I wanted to be in love with a man like my grandfather, all of them.

Roosevelt was the first man I knew existed outside of the doctor who slapped me on the ass and reiterated a gender identity upon me that I'm sure aided in what would feel like my oppression. He was a grandfather I would spend the rest of my life getting to know and training myself after. He made it easy for me to be exactly who I was. He was invincible, and for so much of my childhood, I knew that he would last forever. I knew that men were not Barbies and couldn't be equated to them, but somehow, I wanted to put him in a box, dress him up nicely, and save him for the moments that were hardest in my life. He understood me in ways that most black men would never allow me to understand myself. He stood at about six feet tall and had the most piercing, brown, and grey eyes. I always thought it was weird but never mentioned it to him because a part of me always thought it made him special.

My grandfather and everything about him were always special. The way that he was able to get up every morning and build buildings, and then come home and make the most fantastic food you could have ever tasted. It was nothing short of a magic trick. He was Houdini, for the lack of a better word. And my brother and I were his loyal subjects; we paid for tickets every night to see what we felt was the most prime example of a man.

Beyond being a hard worker, he taught us how to love fiercely. The way that Roosevelt loved my grandmother was truly unmatched. He showed us that love was friendship and that without it, love was also impossible. His beard was scruffy, and Roosevelt often kept his hair cut low. He reminded me of a black Santa Claus if that was ever a thing. Only Roosevelt was much more in shape. And instead of a red suit with white fur trim, he may have been spotted in a pair of steel-toed work boots and a classic FUBU original work shirt and whatever jeans or cargo pants he could find. Roosevelt was indeed my hero. He knew what manhood was. But what made him special was that Roosevelt never spent a ridiculous number of times trying to get me to see manhood through his eyes. He would always take the time to let me find my footing, even when that meant I would fall.

I'll never forget the first time I fell. I recall it almost every other day. I had to be about ten years old, and I lived in a pretty rough part of what most folks would call the "ghetto." I lived in a neighborhood that we all lovingly referred to as "P-S-U." I never found out what those letters meant. But colloquially, all of the kids in the neighborhood agreed that it stood for "People Sweat Us." This phrase is the silliest thing to me now, but the ten-year-old version of me would have gone to war about a housing project built to keep black people in and remind white folks to drive faster if they ever happened upon this neighborhood by accident.

On this particular day, I found myself at the new playground they had put, smack dab in the middle, of our little slice of Miami heat. I was running around with a few friends and was excited to be one of the first kids that got to test out this new jungle gym equipment and swing set. Everything was going so beautifully until one of the twins from a couple of doors down decided that he had had enough of me "prancing around like a sissy." He pushed me off of the swing, and although every bone in my body wanted so badly to push him back, I did nothing. I said nothing. And I went home. I went to the person that was supposed to protect me—the black man that was supposed to be my superhero.

The only image of men I had outside of my grandfather was the men I saw on television. We all know that for the most part, in the nineties, the only men we saw on television didn't look like my grandfather, which means that their methodology to raising a black boy was nothing like my grandfather's. And I was about to find out the hard way. I went into the house covered in sand on the left side of my body, as sweaty as I could be, lips stained with a lollipop that I had been sucking on earlier, and my knees slightly bloodied from when he pushed me. I gave my grandfather an exact look that I'd seen Jessica Biel give her dad on "Seventh Heaven" whenever something happened, and she needed his help.

The only difference was I wasn't Jessica Biel, and this was not a white, suburban neighborhood. My grandfather was not a middle-aged white man who believed in turning the other cheek or letting God figure it out. And so, the reaction that I got was nowhere near the one that I expected or wanted. As I looked him in the face and told him what happened, before I could finish my story about how he had pushed me or even show him my mildly scarred knees, he was rapidly moving me out of the door and back to the same playground where the very same set of twins was now swinging in my place. He pushed me inside the gates, and from the outside, I remember him yelling frantically, "If those are the boys who pushed you, then you're gonna fight them and push them back!" One of the twins decided that he wanted nothing to do with the fight. He opened the gate to the playground, a space that was once festive and fun, and then closed it, locking the little latch behind him.

What started as a day on the swing turned into a miniature deathmatch, and I was the star. I had never been in a fight before at this point in my life. I had never even had to show aggression beyond mild tears for being reprimanded for something I had done personally. So to be in the middle of a fight in broad daylight as other kids gathered around to watch the show made me feel like I was about to throw up. But, I also wanted to prove to my grandfather that I could be a man and that I could be just like him. And so, before anything else could happen, I threw the first punch. I swung and barely hit the twin, who had a look of sheer enjoyment on his face. I could tell that this wasn't his first close-caged match. He was experienced. He knew what he was doing. He understood the rules of this part of manhood. He understood what it meant to be a black boy. He understood what it meant to prove that you could be a black man, and he also understood that this was my first time. And like so many first times, this was going to hurt. And he reveled in it. He reveled in the thought of making me look foolish. He reveled in the idea of making me cry in front of the entire neighborhood and embarrassing me in front of the one man that I would never want to feel embarrassment in front of, ever.

As I continued to swing frantically with my eyes closed, I remembered telling myself that if I kept swinging, even if I weren't hitting anything, it would soon be over. I kept telling myself that Roosevelt would come and save me if I started to get beat up too severely. But he never did. He let that boy beat me up as the other kids in the neighborhood gathered outside of the gate and laughed. I guess the only good news about this was that camera phones hadn't been invented yet. So, the only way that people would hear about this story would be if someone told them. And I never intended on telling anybody. We fought for what seemed to be hours, and everything started to move in slow motion. I watched the room, the world, and the playground spin around me, every so often catching a glimpse of my disappointed grandfather, who still would not save me, even after I broke down and finally mustered up the strength to scream for his name. I remember after about five minutes of the hours that it felt like I was enduring this beating, one of the moms in the neighborhood decided that she had seen enough, unlatched the gate to the playground, and pulled me out.

Roosevelt grabbed my hand and pulled me inside the house. With tears in my eyes, before I could get up the stairs to the bathroom, he reminded me that every time that I ran from a fight, he would be there to push me right back out that front door. I had no idea why or how someone who was supposed to love me (so) would deliberately put me in harmful situations. I had no idea why or how that was okay. But I do know that the next time that I was forced off of the swings, instead of running into what were usually the loving arms of my grandfather, I would keep my pain to myself, rinse off my knees, and find another spot to play.

That was the first time that I realized that trusting a black man could cost me what felt like everything. It was the first time that I didn't wholly trust Roosevelt in my entire life. It was the first time I understood what it meant to be let down by a black man. And it was the first time that I realized that maybe being a black man wasn't all it was cracked up to be. Perhaps understanding this entire organizational body of manhood was just a cheap trick. Maybe, it was just a compilation of expectations that I would never be able to fulfill. Because I was in a body that didn't belong to me, and I had no idea.

Roosevelt reminded me every single day that I had the option to be who I wanted to be. But he never let me forget that I had a couple of different charges on my head. I was a black man. I was gay. And I lived in less-than-optimal conditions, which meant that I had to understand what manhood looked like in ways that other folks would never be able to. I had to program my mind to understand what it would mean to be legitimate in a community that didn't value men like me; that didn't appreciate little boys who would grow up to be men like me; who didn't see men like me as men. Roosevelt reminded me that the Coliseum gates would constantly be thrust open in hopes of executing little black boys who would grow up to be black men like myself. And that if I weren't careful, I would be fed to the hungriest of lions, and the crowd would scream and cheer as it chewed through my flesh and bones, making room for another warrior. All this was from a black man who fit the mold and understood what it meant to be a black man in our community. And what it meant to grow up black in this space.

Roosevelt never questioned whether or not I could do it, but he often wondered about why. Why did I have to be different? Why did I always have to go against the status quo? Why couldn't I just be like the rest of the boys? One day, I would be able to answer that question. But at ten years old, I had no clue. As I grew up, I learned that Roosevelt wasn't the only black man in my life whose opinion mattered. I started to realize that there was more to this story. I began to learn that I had to consider the source. Consider where my thought process was coming from. I had to outsource and figure out whether or not Roosevelt was the only version of a black man that I wanted to aspire to be. And so, school is the place where I found solace and began my new understanding.

I would take a little bit of something from every example I could get—teachers, other kids, and even the man who dropped off the bread to the cafeteria on Mondays. I would pick up something about manhood from every single one of them, and I would build my stairway to manhood. I would develop my expectations, and I would do so in a way that would create a bubble around me—one that would protect me from the expectations that I couldn't fill and the people who didn't believe in me. However, one that would help me see what I expected of myself and who I was supposed to be were two completely different people. And one of them would have to get used to being alone.

CHAPTER 2:

DADDY ISSUES PT 1

So, many people who understand what it means to be a black man, or to be a man in general, will say that your relationship with your father is one of the most important relationships you can build. My relationship with my father was interesting. Marc Queen Raymond was a Haitian-American black man. And I loved everything about him. I loved my father's beautiful locks. I loved my father's great style. I even loved how his weed smelled when we would ride around in his old, beat-up car. There was something about my dad that, like most people, just couldn't be matched by any other dad in the world. He was amazing. My dad made me feel like I could conquer the world. He was a boxer and just a little over five feet ten inches. But there was something safe about him. I constantly found safety in my father—even though he wasn't around because he and my mother couldn't bear to stand more than five minutes in a room with each other.

When we did spend time together, it was always magical. My dad would come every weekend or whenever my grandmother could get my mom out of the house long enough for him to take me somewhere. And we just went for a ride. Most of the time, I drug him to one of my favorite spots when I was younger, Burger King. I loved Burger King so much that he threatened that I would turn into a chicken sandwich one day, which was my favorite thing to eat. An Original Chicken Sandwich, extra hot, heavy mayo, cut in half, with onion rings instead of fries, and a Dr. Pepper with no ice. My dad knew my order like the back of his hand. And he also knew that if they had cheesecake, limited edition, he had to get me at least two. It was always too sweet for his mouth, but it worked just fine for mine.

My dad wasn't perfect. And frequently, I wondered why I couldn't go and live with him. But I knew one thing about Marc, and it was that he was never ashamed of me. Marc may have said something or done things that put me in spaces momentarily. And a lot of that might be because he wasn't my full-time parent. But my dad never once gave me the impression that he wasn't proud to have me as a son. He even bought me my first Destiny's Child album. Granted, I wished that I had made a better choice because I asked for an album of remixes instead of an actual album. However, as a black man in the hood, when your black son asks for a Destiny's Child album titled "Bootylicious," most black fathers wouldn't think twice about buying it. However, not my dad. He made sure that I had the album and that he got it to me no matter what.

My mom happened to be at home when my father brought the album to my house. And things took a turn for the worst. I remember my dad came early that morning to ask me if there was anything that I wanted. And specifically, in the back of my mind, I knew that I had to have that album. I ran downstairs, and I jumped into his arms. My grandmother sat on the couch with my grandfather, watching a movie while my dad and I talked. Ultimately, I could spit out what I wanted, and he told me that he would be back later with the album. By the time my father made it back, my grandmother was in the kitchen cooking. My grandfather had stepped out to get some supplies for the meal. And my mom had randomly made a trip back home to pick up whatever she needed before heading back out for the day. And for some reason, this was the worst timing possible.

My dad knocked on the door, and there was something about his knock. There was something about his presence. I always knew when he was around. I could sense it. From the moment the knocks rang on the door, I knew that it was my dad, and I knew that this would be trouble for a couple of reasons. My mom and dad, once again, couldn't stand to look at each other for more than five minutes. And also, my dad was supporting a habit that my mom didn't encourage, which was me loving Beyoncé, Destiny's Child, and anything feminine in the way that I did. My dad was enabling me to become "soft." And my mom didn't like it. When my mom opened the door, you could cut the tension in the entire house with a knife. I remember hearing my dad say, "I'm just here to drop off this for my son," and my mom asked, "Why?" She repeatedly asked why he was there as if he hadn't just explained himself. And for the first time, I remember being upset that my dad was simply just trying to be there. He was just trying to be a part of my life in whatever way he could, and at the time, I felt like my mom was just difficult for no reason. I felt like she was selfish. She was keeping my dad away from me, and she had absolutely no reason to do so. But none of that mattered because she was angry with him. And as long as she was mad, everyone else had to be too. I don't remember much of the conversation that led up to the actual argument. I do remember, however, hearing my CD crash against the pavement outside. I don't know who threw it. I don't know how it hit the floor. I just remember crying. I remember running back into my room and crying profusely. I remember that my mom never even came upstairs to address it, even though I know she knew that I heard it. I know that she knew that I listened to the entire argument. I know that she knew that I heard her throw my CD against the floor. I know that she knew that

I heard her ask why he would buy me something like this. And she didn't care. What she didn't realize was that I cried myself to sleep.

That was the first time that I wanted my dad. I wanted my dad to save me from everything. I wanted him to keep me from my masculinity. I wanted him so badly to be like the white dad that I saw on television. I wanted so badly for him to explain to me why my existence had to be narrowed down into a cycle of never-ending toxicity. I wanted my dad to make it make sense. And I wanted so badly to tell him that I wasn't his son. I wanted to express myself in a way that I knew would get me in trouble if I did it to my mother. But my dad made me feel safe. My daddy made me feel like a princess. And he did it without even trying. Everything that was feminine about me, or off, or made other men raise their eyebrows, were things that made my father smile. He loved my ability to dance and perform. He loved the way that I loved the stage just as much as he did. And he loved the fact that I was so passionate about Beyoncé. He never once questioned why she was my favorite celebrity or why I've spent so many hours learning choreography to her music videos. He only supported me as a performer. And quite frankly, when he could, he was the only person that would come to any of my performances or shows. My dad wasn't all good, but he wasn't all bad either.

When I was about thirteen, I finally came out to my mother. And while that conversation wasn't the easiest, and was sparked out of fear, the conversation that I subsequently had to have with my dad was a lot more lighthearted than I expected it to be. I had heard so many stories about how black men were supposed to deal with homosexuality. I had heard so many stories about how masculinity would be policed by your father, and he rejected it if it showed up in any other way than the ones that were already deemed acceptable.

I was visiting my father over the weekend, and I had already had the conversation with my stepmom, Amy. Amy was a Cuban woman with a fire engine for hair and these hazelnut-brown eyes. She was almost as frail as what one would think a stereotypical librarian would be if only that stereotypical librarian had been a stripper in a past life. And she was my confidant. If I couldn't tell anyone else anything about me, I could tell Amy. And she always reminded me that everything would be okay. She was always in my corner. And so, after telling her that I was gay, I remember the look of terror in her eyes when I said that I wanted to tell my father.

We both waited up until about two in the morning. My dad was doing a studio session working on one of his latest mixtapes (yes, I had one of *those* dads). My dad finally got home around two-thirty to find Amy and me sleeping on the couch, with Dave the Barbarian playing in the background. He seemed tired, but for some reason, mustered up enough strength to smile and hug me and ask me what I was doing up. I told him that I needed to talk to him, and it was as if he already knew what I was going to say. My dad sat on the couch next to me, and a sleeping version of Amy, and told me that he would love me no matter what I was, who I was, or how I loved. And that if I was going to say to him that I was gay, I didn't need to make a big announcement of it. My dad became a little bit more of my hero that day. My dad was a weekend parent who knew very little about the entirety of my existence or experience. But the one thing that he did know was that he didn't want to jeopardize what it meant to be in my life and have access to me stripped away based on his understanding of what masculinity was supposed to be. My dad knew that accepting me meant more than rejecting the idea of who I was going to be as a person. And he was willing to support that. Beyond his thoughts, he was ready to help me.

CHAPTER 3:

TRADE (THE SILENT ARRANGEMENT)

I was seventeen when I was introduced to a term so nuanced it would shake my core to this day. "Trade" has a multitude of definitions based on who you're talking to and how their walk fits into the puzzle we know as the world. I was a freshman in college with a new head of braids and makeup skills that would make even the most novice drag queens turn over a new leaf. There in the middle of Montgomery, Alabama, I found a tribe of gays with enough patience to show me the ropes. These boys weren't always my cup of tea, and quite frankly, they weren't even always the best people, but they made me think. They tested my ability to be myself in a space that said I should be like everyone else. These gay black men were different from the ones I'd met back home in Miami.

They all seemed to have old souls no matter how young they were, and none of them craved love as much as I did. I wanted these black men to show me that it could be loved in my body the way I saw on the Internet or TV. Hell, even "Jerry Springer" would do. At that point, I just wanted something that shattered the earth around me but left my soul intact. I wanted to be broken how James had broken me sans the numbing heartache that still gives me the occasional chill.

It was the first summer of my college career, and "The Gays" had already given me an entire year's worth of training on how to sniff out trade and what to do when encountering one. I knew how to play it cool and to keep a secret. I knew that indulging in trade meant that I was holding on to an esoteric contract made by the sheer understanding of what it means to deal with a black man who's sometimes perilously unaware of his ability to be free in his attractions to people outside of cis (assigned female at birth) women. Being with trade is like signing a sexual deal with the devil that you go into hoping you can help mend his wings and float back to salvation, only to realize that you've been hoodwinked and there is no one other than yourself to blame.

Being with trade is the ongoing prosecution of your instinct versus your actions in a court case you'll never win with a jury who doesn't show up but wouldn't vote in your favor even if they did, and so you hang. And as you dangle there for the world to see, he watches. He may even shed a tear or two, but his manhood and hetero-simplicity will always be more valuable than the love you all share. This is all written in the fine print of "the contract" you signed when you opened up the app, got into the car, made eye contact for one second too long, or simply entertained what you thought was a friendly conversation with one of your cousin's homeboys.

Trade is a man, either young or old, who enters into relationships no matter the nature with folks in the gay and trans community that directly benefit them with no regard for the emotional, mental, or physical strain it can have or the toll it may take on the other party. Trade is a man who seeks to trade his dirty laundry and most authentic versions of himself with you as a means to play seamstress to his old Easter suits, blissfully unaware that you've got your seams to rip and hems to mend. Trade is the boy in the back of the class that still thinks that saying "I hate you" is the best way to gain your attention, knowing all the while that he'll get it because part of you hates yourself. Trade is the father of a son who would rather die before he allows his baby boy to be anything like him while thrusting every inch of his manhood into your body and having no remorse in some cases for expecting you to return the favor.

Trade is the man you love that will never say it the way you need to hear it. He will be the man who will plan an elaborate scheme to meet you at 1:00 a.m. but wince at the thought of meeting you for lunch. Not because you're embarrassing, but because he's afraid he won't be able to hide it. The joy you bring him and the comfort he feels in himself when he's around you. He's afraid that his peace of mind will get the best of him, and for two seconds too long, he'll forget where he is and what you are. He's afraid that you'll remember that you're worthy, and that is his biggest fear because it's his most valuable trait!

Trade knows that to love him, part of you has to loathe yourself, and they sit on the privilege of knowing that the coward in them never has to be discussed because of it. And so they wait. And you wait!

CHAPTER 4:

SPIDERMAN

As far as trade goes, I had a run-in with my fair share of them. I'd like to think that college was my experimental phase. The place where I found the woman that I would become, even though I had no idea that I wanted to be a woman yet. The black men that I met, no matter their sexual orientation, always reminded me that I had one duty: to be a man, be black, and then die. They reminded me that no matter what kind of a man I was, my duty was still to prove to the world that black men were proper. Regardless of how I saw myself in the paradigm of what it meant to be a man, I had to come to terms with the fact that at least at that point in my life, they were right.

In one of the most unconventional ways, I met Quan in one of the roughest times of my life. It was the summer of my sophomore year, and I had decided that I wanted to have what the millennials like to call a "hoe phase." I joined every dating site and app there was. I spent countless hours explaining to men who I was, what I was, and that I only wanted sex. It became a habit for me. I saw it as a game. I decided that I would put aside my morality to become a person that I wasn't comfortable with for the sake of soothing a discomfort that I would never find comfort in. I would never find comfort in what we would classically call "being a hoe." I would never find comfort in jumping from man to man, or sexual experience to sexual encounter to sexual exploration. But what other choice did I have? Honestly, I spent so much of my life policing myself and trying to be perfect. I spent so much of my time trying to pretend as if I wasn't a sexual being. I spent so much of my time loving one man at a time and giving everything that I had. I spent so much time locking myself away in a proverbial tower and then begging for men who never put me in them to climb my hair and stay with me. I didn't want them to get down. I didn't want them to free me. I wanted them to want to be where I was. I wanted to be enough. And if I couldn't do that, then I was going to fuck my way through my feelings. It was going to become my worst nightmares. And I was going to do it until I got tired.

And then, one day, I ran into a man who made me change how I felt about being tired. On one of the many dating sites that I decided that I was going to conquer, there was one, in particular, that shall go unnamed, that almost always got me the attention I was seeking. One of these days, I mustered up the courage to send a message that was so blunt and direct that it should have come with a TV-MA rating. It was the most forward I think I had ever been at that point in my life. I saw a man who looked like everything that I liked. He was mysterious but beautiful. I could tell. He had these great lips and these sexy arms, and his eyes were slightly covered. I remember looking at that profile picture and saying to myself, '*I want to be fucked by this man.*' I wanted this man to take control of me in ways that I have never been controlled before. And I am willing to do anything to get it.

I remember looking at that profile picture and feeling fear, but also excitement. I remember typing up my message click-by-click. It was a short sentence, but the power that I thought I was taking over my sexual existence made it feel like the longest novel ever written.

The message simply said: "Can I suck your dick?" Without hesitation, and what seemed to be an instant response, the mysterious man with the spider tattoo on his arms and the beautiful lips, responded "Sure." After about five minutes of shock that he even responded, I got a second message. The man had gone through my profile and noticed that there was something different about me. At this point in my life, I wasn't yet trans, but I was most certainly not a man. And he knew that. His "sure" turned into "I'm sorry, that's not my thing, but we can still talk if you would like." That conversation turned into another discussion and then another conversation. Before I knew it, I had spoken to this mysterious man with the spider tattoo every single day that week. And then, out of nowhere, nothing. No more responses, no more messages. It's almost as if he ceased to exist. But during the period of our conversations, I realized that I didn't need sex. I needed a friend. I wanted somebody I could talk to and be myself with, somebody who might not have gotten my complete existence but who saw me as an individual worthy of getting to know. I had no idea what this man's name was for quite some time. And to be honest, it didn't matter. We spoke to each other as if we had been friends forever. We talked to each other as if the world stood still for every single one of our conversations. And it happened almost immediately.

After about a month went by, I got a message. It was a mysterious man. And this time, I was not about to let him get away. I remember the night that he reached out. I had come in late from one of my rehearsals with the theater department. It was about eleven or twelve, and I was famished. But as a broke college student, I had no food in my room, and everything I could get to on campus was already closed. Essentially all I had was a bottle of water and a bag of Lay's potato chips. And it didn't seem like something I should be doing at the time, but I was desperate. So I told the mystery man that I was hungry, and like the gentleman that I would soon find out that he was, he offered to bring me food. Although we had spoken for a week consistently, we had about a month's worth of hiatus and dodged the natural chemistry. I made the decision that any other teenager in college who was being stupid and making irrational decisions would make: I agreed to meet him at a gas station just a little while away from campus. I had no idea what to expect. I just knew that I was afraid. And so, gathering all of my caution and gumption, I put on my most feminine-smelling perfume, threw on what I felt represented me in the most feminine ways, and then packed away an army knife that one of my straight guy friends had given me. And I marched halfway across the campus to a gas station that was pretty much deserted at that hour.

When I got near the gas station and saw the car that he had described, my heart started to race. I had no idea whether or not I was going to encounter a rapist or if this man would try to harm me. I read so many stories about the men who would get on apps and specifically seek out people from the LGBT community and do unthinkable things to them. And here I was, in the dead of night, away from my college campus and the safety of campus police, meeting up with a strange man who I had no idea about. And for some reason, I felt so safe. When I got to the car and opened the door, I was reluctant to sit in the seats. It was a beautiful, black car, really homey and cozy, and he had the music turned down to a level that felt almost ominous. He looked at me up and down, and I could tell that there was confusion in his gaze. We both examined each other like we were science projects. I could tell that this was new for him, and it was new for me. He gave me the Taco Bell bag. I checked the order to make sure that everything was correct and then made a joke about how he was a man that listened. After we sat in the parking lot of the gas station, somewhat exposed by the lighting, after about ten minutes, he offered to drive somewhere else that was a little bit more secluded. My stomach dropped to the pit of my groin, but something in me allowed him to pull off. Something in me allowed me to feel safe with a stranger; allowed me to be taken by the way that he smelled, or the way that his locks laid across his shoulders, the way that his jeans fit his thighs perfectly, and the way that his shirt hugged his unique arms. Something about him made me feel like I knew him.

And so, we drove for about ten minutes and found a street near the campus that was virtually empty, and that became our spot. We found this street and made it our place. And for the next year and a half, almost every other day, he would pick me up, and we would go to this spot and talk for hours, sometimes right up until the sun was about to come up. We would talk about everything from school to life, parental issues, and how things were going with me and other guys. I started to fall for this man. Our friendship had become something that I depended on to make it through the day. Our time together had become something that I cherished. I started to value his opinion and leaned on him to help me make better decisions. He was an older man. And while he was a little removed from the ways of the millennial, he understood the tactics that we used to survive in the more progressive times. And he helped me navigate them in the best ways that he could. But it wasn't always sunshine and rainbows. Sometimes, he would forget to remember that I was an entire human being and not just a quirky, androgynous person he had met on an app. But something about our friendship always made him hold himself accountable.

As year two started to rear its head, I remember consciously taking this friendship to the next level. We had had conversations about sex and even shared a couple of pictures back and forth. We even talked about the possibility of having a threesome, which I was definitely against at the time. But it was one of the only ways he was willing to consider the idea, and I knew that. But for some reason, on this particular night, I still mustered up the courage. I wanted to change the dynamic of our friendship, and I was willing to do it by any means necessary. I remember wearing a cute dress that I found at Forever 21 or whatever little cheap store was in the mall closest to campus. I put on one of my cutest wigs and did my makeup all nice. I did all of this to sit in a car with a man who I was starting to fall for, whose name I barely knew.

And just like usual, he came to get me from campus at our usual spot, and we went back to our usual place, and we parked, and we talked. We talked until I was finally able to muster up the strength to just come out and say it. We talked until the tension in the air was so thick that I couldn't do anything else other than say exactly what I wanted. We talked until we made a bet. We made a bet that I knew that I wouldn't lose, and when I didn't, I made him promise that he would kiss me. And when he lost, he reluctantly did so. I remember at first he leaned in and gave me one of the most mouse-like pecs. It was so emotionless and nervous. He was fidgety, and it was the first time I saw him in the space of vulnerability. He wanted to do so much more but was unsure of what that would say about him or this friendship. And I remember slowly pulling his face back in, pulling his face back into mine, and kissing him with every ounce of feeling that I had developed over the last year and a half. I remember being engulfed in his breath. I remember feeling the warmth of his body as he leaned in closer to me. I remember kissing for what seemed to be forever. And I remember him asking, in his stereotypical joke-like fashion, if I was happy. He asked if I was pleased with that version. And I told him, "Yes."

CHAPTER 5:

PEACE AND LOVE

As far as the black men in my life go, James takes the cake. I met James at a time in my life when I felt angry all the time. I met him when I was discovering myself, and I had absolutely no idea who I wanted to be or what my life would be (like) after the next four years of high school. I had so many aspirations based on the things that I had seen on social media and television. But I had no idea how to put those things into action and make them show up in my everyday life.

I was in a new school with new people, and I wanted to reinvent myself. Being the black, gay boy, I had always been wasn't going to foot the bill in this new environment. I had to be better; I had to be my authentic self. I tried every trend and fell into every group before deciding on what or who I wanted to be known for the rest of my high school career. There were so many different versions of myself that I could have presented, so many different black men that I could have been. And for some reason, I decided that I wanted to be them all. I decided that in the courtroom of life, (that) I have got to be the judge and jury. I decided that I got to make the final verdict on how I showed up in the world. I got to sentence myself to either a life of perpetual silence around my true identity or freedom to explore it. And little did I know, I was about to get help from a black man who knew all too well about what it meant to suppress your voice and then find it in your art.

James became my first love, and for the people who have read my first book, you already know the story of how we met. You know about how he swept me off of my feet in his Cosby sweater. You know about how I fell in love with a person who accepted me when I didn't accept myself. But what you don't know is what I learned from that relationship. What you don't understand is the amount of myself that I found through being able to love someone incapable of feeling worthy of the love that I had to give. By the time I was sixteen years old, I knew that I wanted to marry this man. I knew that I wanted to hold fast to the ideals of what it meant to find a high school sweetheart and struggle; struggle through love and acceptance. I wanted to have the perfect(ly) imperfect story to tell at Christmas parties when people asked how we met. I wanted to be able to be a tear-jerker for the adoption agencies as we shopped around in our late thirties, looking for ways to convince folks that we deserved to become parents. I wanted to prove to myself that the love stories that I had seen in all of my fictional places were not only accurate, but they were tangible; they were things that could be realized. And for so long, I just knew that they would be. I knew that if I entrusted myself to love unabashedly, to give of myself unrelentlessly, I would be able to have the life and the love of my dreams.

James McMillan was about five foot eight, and he had the most beautiful smile cradled in a mustache and wrapped in warmth. If there was anyone in this world I would trust with my heart, energy, and life, it would have been him. There were four years of my life where I learned to unlearn the traumas that had been I had been through. There were so many nights that we stayed up unpacking my pain. There was so much time that we spent doing away with what I have learned about masculinity. And so much energy that we spent pouring into the fact that it was okay for me to be exactly who I was going to be. But there was not enough energy put into the person that I was falling in love with. I was falling in love and learning, which I would become for the rest of my life. And James was settling on helping me get there but never actually learning anything new about himself in the process. Looking back at the entire experience now, I feel like a prodigy. I feel like the relationship was a poem, a never-ending sonnet, something beautiful and timeless. And all of the pieces fall together in just the right ways, but you know it's going to end. And so, you use repetition. You use repetition to save it. To savor the moments that feel the most palatable. To taste them again later. To reread the moments that resonate with your soul the most.

My love for James liberated me and shackled him. This experience taught me that black men, at least some, don't value the need to grow within themselves. It taught me how to perpetuate a constant need to maintain balance and power through the ideation of endless love. It taught me that strength was the only thing I was allowed to be infatuated with as a black man. And that if I didn't have it, I would have to force myself to feel as though I did. James forced himself to feel the power that I never asked for, that I didn't need, but that felt good. The ability he projected upon me to help fix my problems and issues made me feel seen while making him feel validated. But at what expense? At what cost do black men give of themselves to prove a point, make everyone around them feel amazing while killing themselves softly to maintain a masculinity complex that doesn't suit every one of them that is not a one-size fit? At what point do black men get to simply say that they want to love you in the way that feels most natural to them? And at what point does that love get to come from a place of vulnerability and sensitivity? At what point does that love get to forsake righteousness and trade-in pride for something sweeter?

I often ask myself if James' coping mechanism around peace and love being the constant answer to all of my problems was just his way of navigating manhood. I often wondered if everything that we were doing was based on the idea of true love. or if, by some stroke of genius, we had managed to make something that was supposed to be temporary feel like a lifelong journey think. I wondered, and sometimes I still sit back and wonder. I still sit back and ask myself, '*What could I have done to support him?*' Was my understanding of black, male existence was that it was okay to allow them to suffer? Had I disassociated men in a way that allowed me to sit back as my lover and a best friend put himself through hell to help me see myself?

CHAPTER 6:

DADDY ISSUES PT 2

Let me make myself clear. When I say that my dad was a good man, I mean that everything I've said about him previously should still be taken beyond a grain of salt. However, growing up, I had a few fathers, each of them played their roles according to the black man's guide on rearing a black boy for the wonders of manhood in summation with blackness.

Roosevelt taught me that tenderness was nothing if I had no fight in me beyond the smiles I was so eager to bestow on anyone willing to share a kind word. He reminded me that not everyone smiling wished well for me and that it is often true that beyond the cracks in people's often misshapen teeth, there usually lived a gold tooth revealing the cunning fox that they were.

It was okay to befriend, but never to be too friendly, especially as a man. Kindness would be used against me as a weakness, which would then be used to defeat me. A man with a broken spirit was a man looking to be taken advantage of. You were either slick enough to play the game or slow enough to get caught trying, and I never wanted to get noticed.

My dad taught me that there was a thin line between love and regret. We often crossed them in search of the other but rarely made sense of the discoveries on the other side. Persistence with your healing was vital, and it meant a lot to him that I healed the parts of me that he knew he'd never heal in himself. My dad always looked for himself, writing down the pieces that made the most sense and spitting them into a microphone, hoping for an audience. He was always just hoping to heal from a trauma that took me half my life at the time to figure out.

When I was about thirteen, my dad took me to visit my uncle at an old car wash that looked out of commission despite the work- ing electricity and twenty middle-aged guys that hung around for access to free Madden and the occasional ice cream truck drive-by. I had only met this particular uncle maybe once or twice at this point in my life, and from the jump, I knew that he and my dad had tons of unfinished business. The sibling rivalry between them was so thick you wouldn't be able to breathe if you blindly stumbled into a room they both occupied. My uncle Bashawn was taller than my father, maybe 6'2" or so, and had a head full of tiny locks. He had this gorgeous chocolate skin and troubled eyes. They looked as if they had seen death a few times and lived to witness it a few more times after that.

Bashawn wore insecurity well. Although he'd never admitted it and my father never said it, Bashawns envy for him radiated like an old heater in a beat-up Honda in '99. They had a love-hate rela- tionship and thrived on competing with each other no matter the reason. They didn't mind creating an excuse to beat each other into submission, and part of me always wondered why. Part of me always wondered why men, especially black men, felt the need to constantly prove who had the most giant dick in the room, sometimes literally! It never occurred to me that I never understood it because it wasn't who I was meant to be. I just took it as a sign to be mindful of the men who felt the need to use me as a means to show off their grit.

I decided way before seeing how my father and uncle functioned that I wasn't going to be part of that number in the musical of life, and I wasn't going to let stereotypes make me feel like I had to.

On this particular day at the car wash, the sun was beaming down, and my dad, Bashawn, and a few other guys with nothing to do decided that they would indulge in a betting match of Madden 2K—whatever year it was. Being disinterested beyond belief, I decided I would use the time to listen to Destiny's Child in the car. A speaker usually only played 2Pac, and my dad's music was being sonically ravaged by the musical stylings of three black women claiming independence and celebrating the deliciousness of their booty. I was in heaven, sitting in the front seat with some chips and a pineapple soda, minding my business with unlimited amounts of black boy joy permeating the air, until I heard a loud boom to my right.

I looked over my right shoulder, and it was of no surprise to me that my father and uncle had decided to make the car wash their boxing gym, and with what had to be about twenty other men around them, not a single one of them intervened. Curses and kicks flew in front of the car window, and punch after punch landed until my father landed one good punch too many, and Bashawn reached for a pocket knife. No one saw him pull it until my dad's face ran red. I sprung out of the car and rushed over to my dad. Bashawn dropped the knife, apologized anxiously to my father, and ran faster than I think I've seen anyone run before. Almost immediately, an ambulance and cop car pulled into the wash, and for me, at the time, it felt like a movie.

I sat next to my dad in the back of an ambulance with what felt like two hundred people watching and the lights from the cop car and ambulance gleaming. I couldn't explain why it felt like such a rush! But it didn't feel that way to my dad. He was quiet and reserved. He knew how to carry himself among the police. He learned to sit still in situations like this. He knew that one wrong answer or assumption of an attitude could be the difference between us going home or not, but he also knew that I didn't know something that he wasn't yet ready to tell me.

After sitting on the back of the ambulance for a spell, a medic came over to check out the cut on my dad's face and ask him a few questions about his medical history. The man checked my father's eyes and ears. He did all the things they did to me when I'd go to get my check-up for school, but then he asked my dad a question that made him go stiff. "Any preexisting conditions I should know about?" Time slowed down, and my father looked at me, then back at the medic and muttered something I couldn't hear. The medic repeated himself: "Sir, any conditions I should know about?" Once again, my dad muttered something that neither of us could hear. One last time, now visually frustrated, the medic asked in a slightly raised voice, "Sir, any pre-," and before he could finish, my father responded, "H.I.V., man, I got H.I.V."

CHAPTER 7:

UNDERSTANDING

You spend an entire portion of your life trying to make it all make sense; you spend a majority of your life just trying to make everything you're told fit into its subjective place. It's almost as if life is a jigsaw puzzle filled with a million pieces, and every year you're given a different section, and it's your job to just make them all come together in this congruent way in hopes that you'll finish the picture. (I think that) When I think about manhood, that's the way that I put it all together. It's a complicated puzzle that's meant to be didactic, but in many ways, it is so reductive, (and) especially when you are a black man. When you are a black man, that puzzle can become the death of you. That puzzle becomes depression. That puzzle becomes an expectation that you'll never fill. That puzzle becomes a part of the systemic idea of what it means to be something you never signed up for.

When I think about all of the black men that I had met in my life. When I think about the ways that they've affected me. From the boys on the block that sat outside the corner stores when I was growing up to the black teachers that I had that shunned me because they couldn't understand how I could reject masculinity and still think I could be significant for the life of me. When I think about my father and my grandfathers. When I think about the coming and going of men in and out of my life, bed, and heart, it makes me wonder why masculinity is seen as a prize? It (just) makes me wonder. It makes me wonder what about masculinity is so special. What about being a man is so unique and magnificent that it's put on a pedestal? It makes me think about all of the trials and tribulations of women and femmes. It makes me think about how we are constantly policing femininity. It makes me wonder why I never resonated with the black men that I met. It makes me wonder why chauvinism and misogyny never appealed to me even before I stepped into my feminine self. It makes me wonder why I never felt like my penis gave me special powers or why I never truly cherished owning one.

There are a lot of nights where I sit up waiting to understand. I sit in my bed thinking about the colloquial meaning of what it means to be a black man, (and) outside of the stereotypes; outside of the lack of understanding; outside of owning the ideals that makes everyone run and hide, that makes the police shoot them down; that makes black men so revered. What else is there (beyond standing at seven feet tall), beyond standing at a metaphorical seven feet tall no matter how big they are? What is it about black men that make the world stop, that makes us all tremble and shake and listen, that makes us put up with their shortcomings, clap at their mediocracy, and overcompensate when they do things that are just kind of okay? What is it about the melanin and the pheromones combined that make us all bow down? I asked myself these questions for a year. It wasn't until I decided to step into my truth. It wasn't until I realized that I knew nothing about manhood and that I truly understood the beauty and the value of the men that I had met.

(You see) I realized that black men carry the world differently. Black men bear the brunt of the pain and the heartache so that black women can thrive. Black men understand that they ain't shit, and they accept it because if they didn't, the reckoning that would befall the rest of the community would probably crush us. And so, while I recognize the faults in the boys from the hood, while I see the chinks in the armor of the guys who are constantly gambling in front of the local community college, while I judge the men that engage in profuse homo- and transphobia, I get it. I get the need to feel like a protector because nobody is there to protect you. I get the need to feel like you have the privilege to not listen. I get the need to feel like you have the right to conquer the world in all forms. I get the need to feel like love should be unlimited to you; I get it. And while I may disagree with it, and while it may not be my cup of tea, I understand. I understand that in some spaces, there are just going to have to be compromised; compromise for the sake of growth, for the sake of empathy, for the sake of being better than they ever expected you to be because they never expected you to thrive.

And so as I recount my journeys, and as I tell the numerous times that I've met black men that had been kind to me, and I weigh them up against the times that they have been mean to me. I divide them by the number of times I've enjoyed their company and then multiply them by the number of times I've seen them smile. I make room. I make room in my womanhood to appreciate the things that I don't understand. I make room in my femininity to love the things that I cannot produce, check the things beyond my compassion, and live beyond the scope of my own volition. I make room for accountability. I make room for atonement. I make room for disenfranchisement and reparations that will never be given. I make room for the black boys that never got a chance to become men because they were seen as too much of a threat. I make space for the black men who are still boys because they never got a chance to live as adolescents. I make room.

I take my time learning from my experiences and priding myself on giving everyone the space that they deserve, not to prove to me that they can be different, but to just be different. To showcase the best version of themselves without the need for my approval or my wax-sealed stamp. (Because they want to, and for no other reason but because they want to). To have freedom and agency to decide what manhood looks like beyond a binary understanding of sports and height and sexual performance. To understand manhood beyond oppression, simplify manhood down to the most fetus-like knowledge, and do so knowing that they have every right. They have every right to claim the things that feel good without shaming other folks into submission. Because even though black men are given so much power over the black community and expected to perform in ways that make us all feel safe, secure, and guided. There is still a misunderstood sense of how they're supposed to exist with themselves, with the world around them, with the women that love them. And so, the reason that I decided to write this wasn't that I wanted to create a dissertative, think-tank space to chastise my experiences but to acknowledge that I wasn't the woman I am today until I met black men.

CHAPTER 8:

LOVE LIKE MATH

There was a clear understanding of where I stood on the spectrum of manhood. A lot of it was based on my interpretation of how I wanted to be seen by men. When it comes to love and relationships, I was always in the space of never really feeling like enough or feeling like there was something I have to prove to be "man" enough to be considered. I always felt like there was something that I had to prove to be "man" enough to be loved by someone who exudes masculinity in a way that I was just incapable of. A large part of my dating life was wrapped around my ability to hide and shield who I was for the sake of being able to find a partner that felt like I was worthy of their time or energy. The time that I spent being complacent with the mediocrity being brought into my life made me numb to the idea that I could possibly deserve more. I convinced myself there was nothing better than accepting that my value was placed in the hands of the men that fucked and not in my recollection of who I was trying to become. That version of me became a figment of my imagination that haunted me both silently and aloud. These truths I had about myself spared me from self actualization at a time where I'm not sure I Would have survived it and provided a safe haven for the men I deemed worthy of my baggage. They became a pleasant distraction that I was willing to play hooky with inorder to make sense of not dealing with the heaping helping of self loathing I felt the need to do in private spaces for the sake of appearing vulnerable to the mirror that held all of my dirty secrets and sleepless nights. I spent so many years and hours agonizing over what I wore, the way I spoke, and the cadence of my voice to please the people I wanted to be recognized (by) the most. I did all this, only in turn to realize that it had nothing to do with a loving relationship; it had everything to do with how I saw myself and how I wanted to be received. And once I realized that I didn't want to be accepted as a stereotypical black male, something had to change. But I didn't want my interest in black men to have to do so for me to be happy. There was a stage in my life where I thought that maybe if I stopped entertaining them, I would be able to combat my fears—either socially or colloquially—with black men. I felt that at some point, if I was able to convince myself that they were beneath me, it would change the way I felt about not being desired because of my lack of masculinity. I was asking the black men I was falling in love with to fall in love with the woman I would become, not the man they could see standing in front of them. And I realized now that that was unfair. I realized that I was pulling a cloak and dagger for a large portion of my dating life, not just over my own eyes but over the eyes of potential partners and people who wanted to love the image of a man they saw before them.

I remember that I constantly policed myself into corners. Never truly understanding who I was and what it was that I needed, but more so trying to figure out (what or) how to make things flow cohesively in a way that worked not only for myself but for the societal understanding of what I was supposed to be. I realized that so many things were wrong with me, and tackling them would take an entire village, or at least that's what I told myself. I told myself that there were so many things wrong with me that I didn't have to do the work. The scary work. The work that (just about) every person seems to dread, which is the idea of holding (black men) publicly accountable for their actions. I didn't want to say what needed to be told because I was afraid it would make me a pariah. But I knew if I didn't, I would continue to risk my body, emotional health, mental health, and possibly even my life at the hands of people who were even more denounced from themselves than I was. I started to become the type of black man that did what he wanted to do. I began to dress the way I needed to wrap. I started to speak in a way that made me feel most comfortable. And I began to give less of a fuck about who didn't like it. I began to care less about the people who judged and ridiculed me while navigating their own implicit bias. I began to think and weigh out my options: I could either be myself or die. And once I gave myself those options, the answer was clear. And I think that that's what saved me. To be clear, desirability didn't keep me. My understanding of them helped me maneuver my safety in a way that gave me a surefire way to maintain my existence. Because until then, I was basing my sole existence on the approval of the men that I could secure romantically. I was basing my existence on whether or not they thought that I was beautiful or if they could compliment me on things outside of my body. I was establishing my presence on whether or not I could emotionally spar with them for longer than I was supposed to be based on the idea that black women are supposed to endure pain at a higher rate. I was establishing my existence around my self-degradation to not upset the status quo; for the sake of not wanting to make black men look within; without realizing that at the time that I was also a black man who was cloaking myself in an invisible armor to shield my ego from the trauma that I was causing my existence.

And so, I sat up every day thinking. I sat up every night, contemplating, trying to understand what I would do next and how my next move would affect everything from that moment forward. I changed the way that I ate and realized that I was doing that for a man. I changed how I presented myself and then realized that I was doing that for a man. I changed how I spoke about specific topics and then realized that I was doing that for a man. And then, finally, I realized that everything that I was doing was for the acceptance and approval of the black men that I was seeking to be engaged with. And that was until I was able to admit that to myself, I would be in a constant loop. I would be in a constant state of perpetual insanity: doing the same thing and expecting different results. And I had to ask myself: *'Is that what I want?'* I had to truly challenge my ability to be with myself and, finally, get the answers that I needed without the guidance of my wants to lead me through the metaphorical math equations of life. This was not a situation where I was going to figure out that two plus two was four. This was an moment, and I hadn't even solved for the first E., And it was no one's fault but my own. It was no one's responsibility but my own. And I had to do my best to ensure that there were no repercussions for anyone but me.

CHAPTER 9:

RIGHTS OF PASSAGE

So, let's be honest. When I think about whether or not I truly cared about ever being one of the boys, the answer to that question is a resounding "I'm not sure." I made it my business to spend most of my adolescent youth figuring out ways to piss off the status quo for what it meant to be a man. Into my teen years, I decided that I would do more damage by stepping into myself, my entire self, my feminine self, at every chance that I got. I was going to embody my manhood in a way that would piss people off and make folks wonder. I was going to incorporate my manhood in a way that would absolve me of the crimes that plenty of cishet men were constantly accused of. And I was going to do so in a way that made them question their understanding of masculinity.

During my freshman year at Alabama State University, I remember getting myself into what could be described as nothing less than a bit of a pickle. In an attempt to make a point at a historically black college, I decided that I was going to go to a forum that was held by Alpha Phi Alpha, which is a fraternity known for uplifting men within the black community, but also for its stereotypical tropes of what it means to be a man, behave like a man, and look like a man. I wanted to go to this forum because I wanted to prove that I could still be a part of the boys club regardless of what I looked like or what I was wearing. I could still add in much-needed texture to their rigid suit lines. I wanted to prove that my tutu and braids didn't deprive me of understanding masculinity. It helped to amplify it. And so, on this random day in the summer, I decided that not only was I going to go to this forum, but I was going to be as gay as I could be. I had my hair braided in a fishtail pattern, hanging over my right shoulder. I did my makeup with this horrible, blue eyeshadow and pink lipstick combination that would make me vomit if I saw it on myself today. And I even put on a crop top, a tutu, pink leg warmers, and a pair of pink Adidas. I wanted shock value. I wanted them to judge me. I wanted them to look at me and ask themselves a million times over why I had even decided to show up. I wanted them to be uncomfortable. And I could tell as I made steps toward the fraternity house that the forum was being held in that, interestingly, precisely what I was going to do.

My breath quickened, and all I could hear was my heartbeat as I got closer and closer to the house. Mainly because I could see other black men on campus venturing into the house; however, they all seemed to know something about this space that I didn't. They were all wearing suits and carrying binders as if they were there to take notes. This wasn't a regular forum; something was up. And I had no idea, at least until my friend at the time, Chris, walked up to me before I could get to the front steps and said: "Are you crazy? You know that this is an entrance meeting, right?" I had no idea what an entrance meeting was, but apparently, many fraternities and sororities would use the words "forum" when they meant audition. Entrance meetings were places where folks who sought out the opportunity to be in the fraternity or sorority could go and peacock to be chosen for that year's line. And I had just infiltrated the space unbeknownst to myself. But at this point, it was too late. They had already seen me, and quite frankly, walking away would have been more embarrassing than the embarrassment that I felt by going in. And so, I decided that against my better judgment, I was going to sit in a room full of suited men with my legs crossed, my hair braided, and my tutu sparkling.

Although my presence unsettled many of the men in the room, they had bigger fish to fry while trying to look and sound impressive. And so the focus shifted back and forth between the weird androgynous boy in the corner and the men who held their future in (and?) the fraternity in the palm of their hands. As the questions started to pour in from the members of the actual fraternity, I remember just telling myself that all I had to do was be the most competent person in the room. I remember raising my hand for every question. I remember that all of the men in the room, even with their suits and their ties, even with all of their amazing haircuts, and their smell goods, and their cis-heteronormativity, had no idea what they were doing. They knew that this was an entrance meeting, and they came expecting entrance, yet none of them were prepared. They weren't ready to answer basic questions about blackness. They weren't ready to answer basic questions about politics or how we could fix the black community. They were only prepared to look the part. They were only prepared to get the title to reap the benefits of all of the things that come with being Greek. They were prepared to live the life of the college guy who gets the girl because of the letters that say something about him. But they weren't ready to be the man that defined who they were before the letter. And so they sat. They sat there quietly as I answered question after question after question. They sat there in awe that this *thing* could be so bright. They sat there, and they listened to me dissect blackness without throwing masculinity under the bus. They sat, and they watched me examine the politics of how we were being treated without blaming anybody else except supremacy, and they did so quietly. And I felt so good; I felt respected and seen. I felt revered and feared. I felt powerful. Because I felt like they were stupid. Even though I knew there were so many intelligent men in that room, I knew that I was brighter than every single one of them that day. And something is interesting about the way that my humanity showed up. Interestingly, I chose to integrate who I was with who they expected me to be in that space. Something was interesting that no matter what I said or how well I articulated it, they would never take me seriously.

I recall the meeting ending, and all of the men who came "prepared" left with their heads slightly lower than they were when they walked in. I remember the chapter president asking me to stay back as six of their men sat in the room, and they all shook their heads and looked side to side toward each other. I stood in front of them and felt more judged than I had ever felt in my entire life. Six black men I didn't know, who had no control over anything I was doing in life, made me feel so nervous. They made me feel like I had something to prove. And then one of them says, "You know you would be a great candidate if only you could get rid of all of *this* stuff," he said, referring to my outfit. And I remember without thinking twice about it looking at him and saying, "But even with all of *this* stuff, I answered more questions, I presented more facts, and I knew more information than every single one of those other men in that space. And so why should I have to change to be a part of a brotherhood that doesn't respect my intelligence because my appearance isn't what they need?" None of them could answer. They all kind of shook their heads, looked over at each other again, and thanked me for my time. But then, they offered me space to always come back and feel free to be a part of the brotherhood if I was ever willing to change who I was to do it. And I simply wasn't. I just simply wasn't.

CHAPTER 10:

NOT MY SMILE

So, when I think about happiness, a large part of me forgets that black men aren't afforded the ability to engage with joy in the way that other people are. A large part of me forgets that Black men are taught to be rock solid. They're taught to be stiff and rigid and to default to fear. Whether it be being the person that creates fear in others or being a person that is fearful of how they are seen by the community, happiness just doesn't seem to be something that is a long-lasting effect on black men. I learned this in large part because before discovering my transness, I was hell-bent on rigidity. I wanted to smile without the lasting effects of joy. I wanted to be happy without the lasting effects of peace. And I wanted to do these things because I felt that they made me more masculine. They made me more of a man. These things made me more desirable and fun to be around, except that they didn't. This idea of being a black man sans happiness just never made me feel complete. And I wondered why there was need; I asked why there was a yearning to be okay with mediocrity. Why was there a yearning to be OK with the idea that my masculinity was so intrinsically tied to my happiness that I was willing to deny myself joy in the long term for the sake of appearing to be masculine?

It brought me back to the countless relationships and men I would meet who could love me and not like me throughout my transition. Who would fuck me and never see me as an actual person? Who could make sense of my identity for the sake of making themselves feel more like a man but could not simply be happy with me? It was very seldom that I was able to find someone who understood what it meant to just hold himself accountable for just being happy with me. I would get small glimpses of smiles. I would get little pieces and tiny droplets of joy, and now and then, I might even find somebody capable of saying that I made them feel good. But then reality would set in, and the four walls of the room that we were consummating whatever our relationship was would fall away. I remember that we were just a part of a show, which would be forever in production but never actually picked up by a network. We were a part of a show that would be a hit if only Netflix would just give it a shot. If only 20th Century Fox and the producers that sat at the writing table would just hear the pitch, this show would be beautiful, and we would both know it. And for some reason, masculinity would keep both of us from being happy.

I realized that as a black trans woman, I hadn't escaped this idea of rigidness. I had only switched positions with the way that it affected me. I now went from being somebody who could inflict this on myself to being someone that it was imposed upon. And I think that it was almost worse knowing that being happy as a black man wasn't celebrated. However, it was something that everybody wanted. It was something that the world seemed to crave. Everybody wants black men to be happy, and they want black boy joy, and they want freedom and authenticity. However, there wasn't a space, and still isn't a space created that makes it safe for black men to be anything outside of those scary things that go bump in the night. That makes it physically impossible for black boys to wear hoodies in Florida. It makes it dangerous for black men to run in their neighborhoods or sell loose cigarettes outside a community corner store. I realized that the jargon we use for happiness was never set up to support men we think are incapable of digesting it. We believe that black men are incapable of digesting happiness, and so, therefore, we deprive them of the ability to give it. We rob them of the ability to understand joy.

CHAPTER 11:

LOVE?

So where do you go after love? I think that that's a question that I've asked myself every single time I've had to discontinue a friendship or relationship or any of the ships that sail in the night with black men. The odd question I have asked myself all these years is, '*Where do you go from here*?' I've had relationships with many men from different backgrounds and multiple understandings of life and personhood, but something is different about loving black men. And something is honorably different about exiting a space of love with black men. There is something so visceral and tight-lipped about losing the heart of a black man. There is something erotic and sensual in a mutual agreement to end things. There is something archaic about understanding the personhood that built something that was supposed to be intangible.

It's funny how we think of feelings as these things that can be felt while acknowledging that we don't know how we feel about them. And I believe that when we tweet out something like #BlackLove and #BlackMen, men throw out things like bible scriptures in the black community for the sake of defending manhood and fatherhood and the sanctity of what it means to be loved by a strong black man, we forget that he is only as strong as his kryptonite. Black men in love are supermen. They can fly around the neighborhood and protect all of the children. They will spin their wheels protecting and serving and loving and sexing. They will give you the shirt off of their back and provide something fierce with only one caveat. And that is that. You are the only person that gets to hold the key that opens the box that covers that big red button meant for self-destruction. You are Lois Lane, krypton, kryptonite, and Lex Luthor, all wrapped into one. And if that isn't bad enough, you refuse to acknowledge your power because owning your authority over the black man who loves you puts him in danger. But when he no longer loves you, when the posts no longer matter, when the ability to care and listen is no longer there, when his will to love you is shattered, when his need to pretend that everything that you do is perfect fades away, and you are forced to sit in your truth, what happens next? What happens when the black man that you love doesn't love you back? Do you retreat to your former self under the guise of liberation, self-exploration, and a newfound understanding of your personhood, or do you crumble? That is because you realize that he crumbles; because you know that through all of the Instagram posts and the dates, and the endless amounts of sex, and the side-eyed post from his new girlfriend, that he's not happy yet. You acknowledge that he won't be able to move on until you've moved on until you've posted your final jab, until you've let your revenge body just become a body until you've decided to sit in your authentic peace until you've made true peace with the fact that this black man wasn't yours. This superman was not meant to be your Clark Kent. And that this time when he visits the phone booth to change his clothes, he'll open it in a new city that you don't have access to, and it'll hurt like hell because you'll realize what you've done. You'll compare it to what he did, you'll ask yourself if he's doing the same thing, you'll convince yourself that he's not, you'll go a week, and it'll be beautiful, and you won't think about him at all, then one of your songs will play, and the saga repeats.

But what happens when you fall out of love with him? What happens when you stop giving your access to the black men who use you up and make you feel inadequate and small and remind you of all the things that you hate about yourself, and every single way, every single day, make strides to just rip you apart while calling it love, disguising it in care, wrapping it in cheap poetry? What happens when you finally choose yourself over the black man, when you realize that Prince Charming has been the evil step-father the entire time, posing as a prince that he was never qualified to be? What happens when you look yourself in the mirror and say, '*I have had enough of being a damsel in distress waiting on my princess gown to be delivered to a ball held by the wrong person?* Does this black man give you grace? Does this black man admit that it was wrong to trick you, lead you on, allow you to fall deeply knowing that he didn't have the capacity or the want or the tools to sustain the love that you were prepared to give? Does he ask for forgiveness or even apologize? And the answer is usually a resounding no. He doesn't. He will usually sit quietly, waiting patiently for you to crack, because as a black man, pride hits differently. Pride says that black love is suffering. His pride says that because you are a black woman, that you can take it. And so, in my case, as a black trans woman, it was assumed that I could take it ten times as hard. Not because I deserved it, but because I was stronger than the other girls. Because I wasn't a "real" girl, and deep down underneath it all, the black men that I wanted oh-so badly to love, the black men that I believed understood everything that I was trying to convey often never truly believed that I was a woman. Because part of me didn't want to believe that I was a woman. And so, what happens when you stop loving a black man, and that black man stops loving you, and neither one of you can admit it? I ask myself this question as I think about the countless number of grandmas and grandfathers who haven't touched each other in years but still manage a feisty friendship for the sake of optics and comfort. I ask myself this question as I think about the number of aunts with twenty-year-old live-in boyfriends who have never even thought about or contemplated the idea of marriage, but we all call him "uncle." I think about this as I think about the countless number of women who have visited ring shops and hunted for dresses waiting on a question that will never be asked. Because the love was either never there or dwindled at some point, we decide to hold on to the fantasy because it makes us feel like part of the high society. It makes us feel like we share something with the white folks that oppress us and do the same thing. It makes us feel like we are in the same shitty rat race, playing the same shitty game of life while opting into a scarcity mentality as if black love can only exist in the one instance that you find it, which we all know isn't true. And so, what happens when you love a black man, and he loves you back? To be perfectly honest, that's something I have yet to truly experience.

CHAPTER 12:

RAINBOW BOYS

Eartha Kitt once said that "A man has always wanted to lay me down but has never wanted to pick me up, and the ones that did have a real affection for me were the ones that never touched me." So, when I speak about finding true love and affection in black men when I think about the happiest moments of my life spent with black men, it's been with the black men that have been tossed out of the hierarchy of what it means to be a man ultimately. I remember the men in my life who, like myself, have been called "fruitcakes," "faggots", and "sissies". Constantly reminded that on the hierarchy of male hood and what it means to be a man and grow up in the black society understanding what the culture says men are to be, these men never fit the bill. The politics of masculinity didn't allow these men to fully engage in the social understanding of the male hierarchy as it pertained to a lot of the men that played in the boys club, that followed all the rules, were not men. But these men were and are and continue to be some of my greatest gifts.

I think about the first day that I met my friend Sky. He was this Lite-Brite high yellow tiny little thing that had the most beautiful smile, shining bald head, and ridiculously banging body. And I was walking back after having dinner at the cafe in my university.

I remember he had his headphones on, and while I was reentering the building, he passed me at first. And then I guess it dawned on him that on this particular day, I was wearing my natural hair; no wigs, no makeup, no extensions or clip-ins, just my natural hair and a little ponytail, and I remember hearing his footsteps abruptly stop before hearing his voice, which I'll never forget to this day, screech out at me "Girl, where is your wig?!" And for some reason, in a space where I would have taken offense had anyone else said it, I allowed this stranger to questioning something at the time was the fullness of my femininity. Something that at the time I felt defined me as a woman. I allowed this stranger the space to question my choice to not wear a wig that day. And I responded with a smile and giggled, saying, "She's in my room." He lifted his eyebrows and then sort of chuckled to himself and said, "Oh, okay. I've just never seen you without it." "Cute," he says. And then he gave me the gay man's finger point of approval, surveying my body up and down before turning around and continuing to walk wherever he was going. And from that day onward, we were friends. I would find that little bald head in any space that I was occupying on campus. I would search for him, and shortly after a couple of days or so, he would search for me, and to be quite honest with you, I'm not even sure how our friendship evolved beyond casual conversations in the cafeteria. I'm not sure how we ended up spending sleepless nights in our dorm talking and laughing about everything under the sun, from school to boys, to our similarities growing up.

I will never forget when he introduced me to Jeffery, our six-foot-five mama bear, or Jaylen, our homely Sinclair from Living Single. I'll never forget how inseparable we were. I'll never forget how protected I felt when I told the three of them that I was trans. And I'll never forget the immediate action they took as black men to make me feel beautiful. Never did they waver, or question my name, or use my deadname. Never did they think twice about who I was. They embraced Hope from the second that I told them that that is who I wanted to be; that is who I was meant to be; that is who I was going to be from that day forward. It is because of those black men—those gay black men, the men who did not want to lay me down or sleep with me or explore their options—it was because of those men that I made it through everything. I made it through some of the most challenging times, the most uncertain times because of these men; men that my culture would look down at and cast out because of who they were; The men that black culture says aren't men. It was because of their protection and their understanding of my womanhood that I was able to graduate. Because of their rigorous correction of others, I reminded folks every day that I am a woman and deserved to be spoken to as such.

I will never forget how I felt sitting inside one of our math classes (the only class that Sky and I had together), and the professor hated me. Not because I was a lousy student, but because I was visibly trans. He hated the fact that not only was I visibly trans, but that he had no choice but to respect it because I had legally gotten my name changed. And so, since he could no longer call me by my deadname since he could no longer overtly assert his power, he would passively-aggressively misgender me. He would ask me questions just so he could call me "Sir" in the process. And at some point, it became dangerously apparent what he was doing. So much so that even some of the most bigoted black students in the class would look at me with pity, empathy, or sympathy. But no one ever said anything, including me. I never said anything, at least not in class. I told Sky about how it was making me feel one day after one of the girls in the class addressed it. After we finished a lesson, she walks over to me, and she says "Girl, you know, I grew up believing what the bible said, but I also don't think that it's right that he does what he does on purpose, and I'm so sorry." And I remember looking in my peripheral and seeing some of the male students in the class agreeing. And then I remember crying to Sky and Jeffrey and Jaylen about it and having a Kumbaya moment that turned into a beautiful brownie-making session slash movie night. And then I recall the next time that we went to that math class. I sat in my usual spot, Sky sat in his usual spot, and the course was going fine until this professor once again did what he usually does and decided to call on me specifically to call me "Sir," and then specifically use my deadname which is not even on the roster anymore. It wasn't even in the system. He looked directly at the attendance system, only to ignore it by calling me my deadname and using the wrong pronouns. And before he could finish his complete statement, I remember Sky said, and I quote, "Excuse me, Sir, can you please stop?" And the entire class was so quiet that you could hear a rat piss on cotton. And the look of pure confusion crossed our professor's face as he responded, "Excuse me?" I turned around, and Sky gave me the most comforting look that I think I've ever been provided by a black man. And then he proceeded: "Every time we come to this class, you make it your business to call on Hope but not call her by her name, and you do it on purpose, and we all know what you're doing, and at this point, it's annoying. So, if you're not going to call her by her pronouns, or use her right name, which is legal, by the way, could you just not call her at all?" The professor was so pissed. But not just because of what Sky said, but because at least half of the class visually agreed. Not just the women, not just the other queer kids, but even some of the men that I had pegged as bigoted and daft. They were all shaking their heads or using body language that showed or displayed agreement. And that professor almost turned cold before asking Sky to leave the classroom. To which he did so effortlessly. Sky packed up his things, and in traditional **Just Jack** from *Will and Grace* fashion, stormed out of the classroom. And I gathered my things as well and followed him. And that was the last time that that professor ever misgendered me or called me a name that wasn't Hope. But it was also the last time that the professor ever called me anything in class. And it was beautiful. That was the day that I realized that Sky loved me. He was my brother. He is my brother and my friend. He was willing to accept the consequences for the lack of my self-protection in a situation where he should have been choosing his education. And he was ready to make it publicly known that he would no longer sit and allow for me to be berated, especially not in a space where I was just there to learn. Sky showed me how to own my ability to speak up for myself in the presence of black men. But he also gave me the hope that I could still experience love and compassion from a group of people who often brought me so much pain.

After graduating college, I spent a couple of years in Texas. And for a while, I didn't have many friends. I would go to work, come home, watch TV, and go to work, come home, watch more TV, and go to work, come home, make a wig, and then watch more TV. And then suddenly, a part of my routine became going live on Facebook nightly. I would get up and just talk about my day. Talk about the things that happened and essentially throw stuff at the wall and see what would stick. I would go live about situations that would occur at Walmart or an idiot that cut me off only to end up stopping at a red light. And now and then, Jason would comment. Jason was a six-foot-six Adonis of a black man. Jason was beautiful, and although he lived in Alabama when I attended school there, we were never really friends. We knew a couple of people mutually and shared space once or twice, but we had never made an effort to talk to one another apart from him doing my makeup one time at the Sephora in the middle of town. And even then, he admittedly was nervous because he had never done a trans woman's makeup before. And I just reminded him that trans women are women, and all he had to do was just my makeup. He didn't have to overthink it or come up with some unique formula. All he had to do was my makeup. And so he did, and I didn't see him for a while. Until one night, after one of my live videos, Jayoccurson pops into my inbox on Snapchat and tells me how dope the video was and how he resonated with it, and that happened for months. We would go back and forth on Snapchat, just talking about different experiences or agreeing with various posts that we would see on social media. And sooner than later, Snapchat became video calls, and the video calls became text messages, which became facetime, which became a friendship. And Jayson became somebody I could unequivocally count on for anything. This man became a part of my brotherhood.

I had drifted away from Jaylen and Jeffrey, but Sky and I had become more vital than ever. And just when I needed it the most, Jason and I also grew a fondness for each other that surpassed this idea of societal understanding. Jason became the boyfriend that I never knew I needed. He became my romantic partner. Jason became my protector, my brother, and my lover. And he did so without ever lifting a sexual finger toward me. Jayson makes me feel beautiful, sexy, empowered and loved every day he walks this earth. And at no point will he ever want to engage me intimately, but we both acknowledge that our relationship is filled with love. This six-foot-six gay man, who understands the value of a hug, understands the importance of just sitting in silence, and understands the value of making a woman feel like a woman, became a staple piece in my existence. He reminded me to remember that not all black men were the same. And that not all black love had to come packaged in cis-heteronormativity. He reminded me that black love could be between a cis man and a cis woman with heterosexual values; that it could exist without the sexual component; that it could exist between a black trans woman and a black gay man who simply love one another; and that it could live without the need to explore sexuality as part of the relationship. He reminded me that black love is not only what we see on the hashtags of Instagram, but those black men are capable beyond measure of accessing it when they are allowed to do so in their way, under their terms.

CHAPTER 13:

NUANCE

Black men have a distinct power. It's almost like an innate nature. There's this thing that they can do. They can monopolize their voices to be anything that you need at any moment. A father can become a brother. A brother can become a protector. A protector can become a lover. And they don't necessarily have to become a different person to do any of these things. All they have to do is make you believe it. And it's not always intended to be manipulative. Sometimes, they simply exist in a world that was built, engineered specifically so that they could thrive in that very understanding. Often, what we don't realize about the black men we encounter is that most of them have absolutely no idea who they are. And so they spend most of their time awkwardly surveying the room, looking for the most confident one of them. They spend most of their time in public spaces gathering information and tissues, hoping to form a bond that becomes muscle, something strong enough to be able to retain information, something strong enough to be able to sustain the weight of their existence. Some of these black men are okay with mediocrity because doing better would require them to trust themselves, and they don't. And so, beyond this innate gift that most of them have to shapeshift and be exactly who they need to be for anyone at any moment, some of them, the majority of the time, will opt to be feared. They decide that being perceived as a threat would be better out of all the things worth being. Being perceived as a threat, something worthy of stiff necks and fast-paced heartbeats, is better than being perceived as love, is better than being perceived as protection. Because fear in a lot of their minds should be protected. Then it hit me: Black men often chose to personify fear because there is no protection for them. There is no hierarchy built to legitimize the needs of black men. And while we as black women do our best, there's just something different about how black men need to feel protection that I don't think anyone has grasped yet. And so, we live in a world and sit in a space where black men have learned to protect each other by teaching each other to be feared by one another, the oppression, and their lovers. while we sit back and allow it to happen. Because as other black folks, black women, and black queer people, we understand that there is nuance. We understand that beyond the color of their skin and the texture of their hair, the folks outside of this community don't need to understand that nuance to be afraid. They don't need to understand that innate thing to be scared. They don't need to see the performance or know about the personification tactics that black men use to protect themselves. They don't need any of those things to see fear. And so, in some cases, the rest of us suffer so that this personification protects the black men that we love for as long as they need to feel protected, even if we suffer because of it. But that nuance tends to show up in ways that don't always make sense. That nuance tends to affect black women in a way that I don't think anyone else will ever understand. I don't think anyone else can ever grasp the magnitude of the game that black women have to play. It is the game of eat or be eaten amongst black men; the game of fear or be feared amongst black men; the game of respect; the game of understanding; and the game of rejection. As black women, we take on so much regarding the livelihood of the black men we meet.

We are trained from the day that we accept womanhood. Our goal is to ensure that a black man, whether romantically involved or just platonically associated with, feels like he can see himself as safe within you, regardless of how he makes you feel. And so when you see a black man, and you notice how handsome he is. He smiles at you and watches you walk around your favorite department store looking for something to wear, for a place that's yet to be disclosed, for an evening that's yet to come into fruition, with people that you've only met once, at a college dorm room party, you smile. You ensure that he knows that you are docile enough to receive his advances. You push your braids behind one of your ears, asserting femininity. And you wait for him to say something small. You wait for him to gesture to the dress that you're holding in your hand, hoping that you'll be able to wear it on your first date with him, but instead, he waits about ten minutes until you're searching for a necklace to wear. And from the checkout line, he notices you again. And this time, you flip your braids to the other side of your body, hoping that he gets a good look at your silhouette. Hoping that he embraces those muscular but ever so soft curves. Hoping that he sees mahogany and honey running through your melanin. Hoping that he can smell the Shea butter radiating off of you. And he gestures with his finger to the very necklace that you're holding, contemplating. And says, "Yeah, get that one." And in your mind, this isn't the choice that you would have initially gone with, but to assure him that you're not willing to be combative, that you're not broken, and that you can follow the lead of a man, you smile and say, "This was the one I was thinking about too! Thank you." And you lean into your femininity, and you shrink yourself. Because that nuance says that we can never appear to be bigger or just as big. And then you take your place in line, and you watch him watch you. And you watch him contemplate whether or not he's going to make his next move. And then, you watch the Latina woman gently stroke his shoulder and ask where he got his jacket. And you realize that the nuance of this situation says that even though she is in her messiest bun, with her most acne-prone face and her dirtiest pair of house slippers, the nuance of the black man says that she is better than you. The nuance of the black man does not care about how beautifully your braids are done. It doesn't respect the fact that you took an extra five minutes to make sure your baby hairs were laid or that you sprayed on your most expensive perfume because you knew that today was going to be the day that you were in the presence of kings. And you wanted them to know that a queen was entering the room before she ever stepped her foot through the door and that she had been there long after you leave. You wanted to be the best version of yourself, and for all intensive purposes, honey, you were. But the nuance of the black man finds protection in the light skin and the loose curls and the soft, pastel eyes of women that don't look like you. And this is not all men. This is not all black men. And you've been prepped for this day as a black woman since the day that you've accepted your womanhood. But the same man that has followed you around your favorite department store and helped you pick out your necklace has now forgotten you exist. And you chuckle, you pick up your phone and text your group chat, and you move on. Because of the protection of the men that we love, the protection of black men requires you to. It requires black women to see that femininity can only be protected if everyone has agreed on its brand. And the one that we walk around with as black women has yet to be FDA approved. And so, we wait for the rarest of opportunities of radical black men that are willing to be the test dummies for our love. The ones willing to become our best friends, our brothers, our protectors, and our fathers. The ones willing to defend our womanhood beyond the need to substantiate their masculinity or manhood or their understanding of what it means to be feared. But until then, we continue to walk around our favorite department stores looking for the dress for the event that we are yet to go to and the perfect shoes for the floors that we have yet to walk, to match with the necklace chosen by the man that we'll never speak to because you haven't learned to understand nuance. I never understood nuance until I met black men.

CHAPTER 14:

PERSONAL PRISON

When I think about what it means to be a black man, I think about the idea of being perpetually locked in cages. I think about the lack of understanding given to the black male simply for existing in a way that he has no control over. His skin color is perceived as a weapon, and his stature being perceived as a threat. I think about his dick being perceived as a barricade and his lack of ability to Define himself as a hindrance; I am constantly reminded as I watch black men maneuver everyday situations and societal mishaps that a lot of them, whether they have been to jail or not, live life like prisoners. They galavant about utilizing the tools of patriarchy to justify their ignorance while also blaming that very same system for the reason why they remain ignorant, understanding that the warden is the societal deprecation of their individuality; however, being complacent enough to never even think about changing that is what's always interesting. The way black men often police one another is a system I've been privy to in multiple spaces. I've watched black men look over one another like prison guards awaiting the yard riot of the year. Monitoring each other's every move being sure to create dysfunction amongst those who find individuality in spaces where individuality it's seen as a weakness. In the prison yard of Life, the black man finds a way to devour himself while acknowledging that he stops being hungry for the normality he's told to think is his livelihood. I've watched the evolution of some black male thought processes, and it's always the same. Some of them enjoy the status quo, while others enjoy playing the role of ignorant brute for the sake of being able to go through life unscathed; they enjoy being able to be one of the boys. They want the boys club. The privilege of putting their thumb on those who are just a little bit more oppressed because it makes them feel like less of a prisoner to the system themselves. And so rather than take the time to explore themselves, they would rather stay in prison and find partners that they feel are suitable, gullible, and naive just to have you sit with them in the cage that they built to protect their masculinity our blackness, and what they deem to be the culture. This is why we have Hip Hop. A space where so many men talk about the woes of what it means to be thrown into the prison system explicitly built to harbor the lives and the energy of Black Folk specifically black men, but none of them realized that as they perform masculinity in the most stereotypical of ways that they give power to the very system that loathes the culture that they've created. They provide power to separatist views, fuel hatred, and make it possible for those who don't understand us to continue to negate our existence, humanity, and personhood. Some black men don't see that from the time that they accept that their fate is to be a stereotype. They make a choice to embolden the system that seeks to lock them all away, not necessarily because they're the strongest, but because they are the most impressionable. Essentially, most black men, when allowed to be themselves, are the weakest link and refuse to see it. Not to mention as the societal need to appear "Normal" When given a choice to stand out, a lot of black men choose to be ominous and singular, to blend for the sake of learning how to convert their own thoughts and personal understanding of the world into something that will make sense for those around them. Never taking the time to understand that every other black man they are trying to impress is just as confused and lost. Never taking the time to ask each other the hard questions about what it means to really be a black man and accepting that everybody will have a different answer, acknowledging that not everyone we'll share a love for misogynoir, patriarchy, sports, sex with women, or being a man.

CHAPTER 15:

THE PATRIARCHY OF PRIVACY

Discretion had been a word that I have been all too familiar with since I realized that my manhood would be shaped differently than the other boys I was being socialized with. I found myself in a space where this word became vexing while navigating all of the dating sites and in-person meetups; this notion of privacy by way of discretion seems to be something that stops black men valued over life itself. Many black men I encountered found themselves above reproach regarding other people's privacy; however, it seems to be the only thing that mattered when commenting on their own. The ability to have privacy while doing something that they deemed to be perverse Seems to be the main objective of black men who, on the one hand with judge folks for living alternatively while I'm the other enjoying that alternative pleasure for themselves in insatiable ways.

I found that some black men have a culture of dominating privacy by making the folks they seek it from feel like it's a privilege to carry their burden. For instance, the married man approaches the vulnerable woman under the guise of a relationship on the brink of failure. They often paint themselves to be a victim in a situation to a person who already feels victimized therefore creating a sense of connection, another way to bond and allow space for their victim to feel they have something in common. After establishing this connection and commonality, they then bestow the burden of privacy on 2 their victim by spoon-feeding it in waves, Emotional manipulation sandwiched between things that feel like love and Trust.

This privacy is a contract between black men and the folks that they seek Solace and. Essentially gives them the right to do away with your humanity and treats you like property, with the nature of your relationship determining what kind of property you'll be. Sexual, intellectual, spiritual, or all of the above. At some point, we've all fallen victim to the black man's privacy clause. Now, this doesn't make us innocent because, at some point, we've all agreed to play our role's to sedate our own demons. Still, we do so at the expense of ourselves and the folks who will encounter the same men we've emboldened, enabled, and exonerated of accountability time and time again in the name of hope.

Hope that we will be different, the one to change the narrative and shift his focus, knowing deep down that you can smell the unrelenting stench of stagnation surrounding his aura. Knowing that you won't even be around long enough for whatever plan you were concocting to be put to use, and yet here you are! Complicit in the patriarchy of privacy that has told you to feel special because you know something about him that you think no one else does because he's said to you that it's a secret. And you believe him and protect it with your entire being because he's often convinced you it's the best and most important thing you can do for both you and him. This is a skill. It is a skill that has taken many intelligent folks to places they never imagined themselves because the heart and the need for sex trump any degree from every university you can ever dream of attending. Regarding privacy, the black man reigns supreme at the ability to run the same game in one space, lose, and win with the same strategy somewhere else.

Privacy is at the discretion of the person with the most to lose. Rather than owning power for black men, most of us allow the chess game to be played to completion and cry about what was then revel in what is. As someone socialized to believe that my dick made me superior, the power of privacy made me feel disgusting. Deciding that someone else feeling about me were null and void because of my inherent social trauma wasn't ever ok with me, and using my stigma as a crutch never felt like a get out of jail free card in the way I think it was mean to. It was scary, and to this day, I'm scared of it. The thought of being asked to keep something private by a black man paints an uncertain picture for me that I'm not willing to finish anymore. This brings me here. To this space on this page in this book in my life where I can both metaphorically and realistically say I've freed myself from the bondage of the black man's secret and pray I never fall victim to it again.

CHAPTER 16:

THE STRUGGLE

When I sat down to create this piece, I thought to myself how many ways I had indeed moved away from something bestowed upon me as what most people would think is a gift. I thought about the ways that people would claim or receive my rejection of this "gift." I thought about how many folks would not understand what it meant to be in this body and how often I've been asked when I decided to become something else. I thought about the number of times people would use the lack of a father figure in the home; the number of times people would ask me, "Which black man has hurt you?" The number of nuances that would go into every word that was written on these pages. And so I wrote. And as I wrote, nothing was good enough, and so I stopped. I repeatedly restarted the pages until I realized that I needed to take my hand off the page, silence my voice, and just listen to my thoughts. In doing so, I remember the privileges of what it means to be able to claim manhood. I understood that my brand of femininity had to be questioned or placed under constant scrutiny because it was foreign, but because so many people had trouble making sense of why you would want to give away so much privilege to be something that people don't respect. In the black community, we honor, uplift, and uphold women as matriarchs of the community. Frequently, our mothers, grandmothers, and favorite aunts are the people we go to for solace, love, and perpetual understanding. But to want to be them, to want to enact that same love in such a personal way, doesn't make sense. And so, when we talk about the nuances of being a black trans woman and navigating a world where black men hate you while wanting to love you simultaneously, we find ourselves amid confusion. We are dismayed by the reality that we know to be true, the one that we live and often have to go through; the reality of all of the backseat car sessions in college, or the number of times that you've had to sneak them in and out of your mother's house as a teenager, or the late nights filled with full faces of makeup, only to have it shoved into a pillow for a five-minute romp around with a man that loves you, but will never be able to say it. And not because he doesn't feel it, but because he's told that he can't. He's told that loving you and loving your brand of femininity transformed him, and it makes him somebody different—somebody he simply does not want to be. And in many spaces, that fear becomes anger, that anger becomes confusion, and that confusion can be deadly. As I thought about what I wanted to put into these pages, I struggled immensely with my decision to speak on abuse. I struggled immensely with telling the story of a twenty-year-old Hope, who was broken, felt lonely, and wanted nothing more than to just feel wanted, beautiful, and loved, even if she knew it wasn't real. I struggled with talking about the night I decided to get onto a dating app and allow a man I did not know. that I was not attracted to, to pick me up from my college campus, drive me to a house that felt like a jail cell, to a house with no furniture, freshly plucked cable wires hanging out of the walls, the scent of paint wafting through the air. I struggled to talk about the faint scent of dog piss ruminating from the back room. Or the way that the windows seemed to be making fun of me as they creaked backward and forward. I struggled to talk about my need, will, and want to run, but I did not know where I would go and had nobody to talk to. I struggled to talk about the sound of his boots against a hardwood floor. The way that the dirt crunched under him as he walked over to me and didn't speak a word. I struggled to talk about how he grabbed my hair and spun me around. He spun me in a tango-like fashion, and for something that happened so quickly, I felt like I was spinning forever. I struggled to talk about the way he pushed me to the floor. I struggled to talk about the way that I couldn't breathe, let alone talk. I struggled with how scared I was or with how I felt like I had no right to say "stop." And so, I struggled. I struggled with saying nothing and feeling like an accomplice. I struggled with crying as he penetrated me using his filthy hands and then simultaneously his wet mouth to lubricate himself and enter me. I struggled with knowing that he didn't care about my tears. He asked me why I was crying, but never once did he stop. Never once did he break the rhythm. I struggled with the fact that he asked me to let him finish. "Just give me a minute," he said. I struggled all the way home. Back to my dorm room, where I scrubbed for hours in a community shower, as the boys who would become men waltzed in and out, reminding me of my struggle. And then I remembered the resilience of my grandfather. I remembered the tenacity of my father. I remembered the love I had received from James, Malcolm, and so many other men, some of them who barely knew me but had fallen in love with me. I remembered what it felt like to be seen, and I buried that struggle. I buried that story because I felt like I had no right to tell it. I buried it for years because I didn't think anybody would care. I buried it into every relationship, into every exchange with a black man. I buried it into my experience as a black woman. I buried it into my history so deep that it began to permeate my thoughts whenever people ask me why I would give up the gift of being a black man. And I was reminded to never admit that that was part of the reason. Because that was a cop-out. And it wasn't until I met black men who wanted nothing from me that I realized I had every right to tell it; that I had every right to feel; that I had every right to cry, ruminate, and fester. But what I did not have the right to do was disappear. And so, I became who I was meant to be. Not because I lacked a father figure or understanding of my situation, but because I could have never been the woman I am without the lessons, the love, and the hardship that I learned from my time as a black man. I learned that I wouldn't be the woman I am today and that I wasn't the woman I am right now until I met black men.